Impetuous arrival...

ON A COLD winter afternoon in January 1965, a *Battle of Britain* class locomotive steamed into Long Hanborough station, the stop for Blenheim Palace, two miles away. It carried the mortal remains of Sir Winston Churchill on their last journey to his chosen resting place at Bladon, just to the south of Blenheim Palace where he had been born 90 years earlier.

Churchill's father, Lord Randolph (a younger son of the 7th Duke of Marlborough) and his American wife, Jennie Jerome, were staying at Blenheim

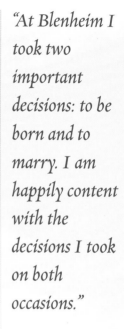

"At Blenheim I took two important decisions: to be born and to marry. I am happily content with the decisions I took on both occasions."

Lord and Lady Randolph, Winston's parents

"The finest view in England."

No.	When and where born	Name, if any	Sex	Name and surname of father	Name, surname and maiden surname of mother	Occupation of father	Signature, description and residence of informant	When registered	Signature of registrar	Name entered after registration

*Registration District **Woodstock***

*1874. Birth in the Sub-district of **Woodstock** in the **County of Oxford***

| 388 | Thirtieth November 1874 Blenheim | Winston Leonard | Boy | Randolph Henry Spencer Churchill | Jennie Churchill formerly Jerome | M.P. for Woodstock | Randolph S. Churchill Father Blenheim | Twenty third December 1874 | George Foster | — |

Registrar.

Palace when Winston was born on 30th November 1874, a few weeks earlier than expected.

The Blenheim influence began in his earliest years. Heir presumptive to the dukedom until the birth of his cousin the 9th Duke's son, Winston was often left in the care of his grandmother at Blenheim while his parents pursued political and social careers in London. The house and its historical association with the achievement of his ancestor, John Churchill, 1st Duke of Marlborough,

ABOVE: *Winston's birth certificate*

BELOW: *Curls cut from the 5-year-old Winston's head*

had a profound influence on the boy. Much later in life, when speaking of the rebuilding of the bombed out Houses of Commons in 1943, Winston commented, *"We shape our buildings and then our buildings shape us."*

Certainly, Winston Churchill was shaped by Blenheim Palace. Built as a monument to the victory of his great

ABOVE: *Churchill's baby vest*

LEFT: *The Birth Room at Blenheim*

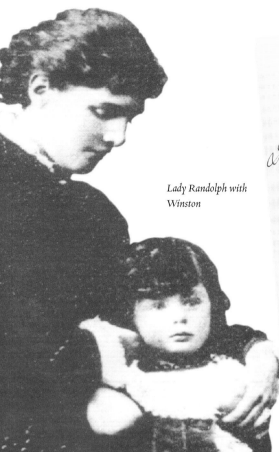

Lady Randolph with Winston

LEFT: *Letter from Lord Randolph to Mrs Jerome on the birth*

ancestor, the 1st Duke of Marlborough, over the French in Bavaria at the Battle of Blenheim in 1704, this majestic building was an inspiration to Winston throughout his life. He describes this awareness himself, a consciousness of centuries of history surrounding him there: "*Roman, Saxon, Norman, Plantagenet, Tudor, Stuart prefaced the 1st Duke's action at Blenheim,*" he wrote.

The Dukes of Marlborough

SIR WINSTON CHURCHILL, 1620–88
|
JOHN, 1ST DUKE OF MARLBOROUGH, 1650–1722
|
HENRIETTA, 2ND DUCHESS, 1681–1733
|
CHARLES 3RD DUKE, 1706–1758
|
GEORGE 4TH DUKE, 1739–1817
|
GEORGE 5TH DUKE, 1766–1840
|
GEORGE 6TH DUKE, 1793–1857
|
JOHN, 7TH DUKE, 1822–1883
|
GEORGE 8TH DUKE, 1844–1892   RANDOLPH, 1849–1895 = JENNIE
|
CHARLES 9TH DUKE, 1871–1934   WINSTON, 1874–1965 = CLEMENTINE
|
CHARLES 10TH DUKE, 1897–1972
|
JOHN 11TH DUKE, 1926–

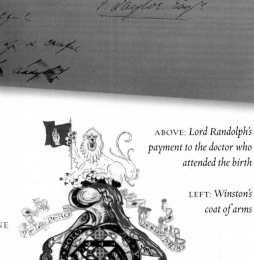

ABOVE: *Lord Randolph's payment to the doctor who attended the birth*

LEFT: *Winston's coat of arms*

Blenheim childhood...

AS A BOY Winston was a frequent visitor to his grandparents' home. At the age of 8, in his first recorded letter to his mother, from Blenheim, he enthusiastically thanks her for the presents of *"Soldiers and Flags and Castle"* – a sign of things to come! Along with his brother Jack and his cousin 'Sunny' (later, 9th Duke) he invented games that the boys would play in the spacious rooms and long corridors of the palace. He did *"lessons every morning"* which left ample time to enjoy Blenheim's other pleasures: riding his pony Robroy, catching fish in the lake and going for drives. *"The gardens and Park"*, he wrote to his mother, *"are so much nicer to walk in than the Green Park or Hyde Park."*

His grandmother, the formidable yet warm-hearted 7th Duchess, understood well the needs of the young boy and grew to know Winston well. By the time Winston was at Blenheim aged 14, the Duchess was writing to Lord Randolph, *"I keep Winston in very good order...he is a clever boy and not really naughty but he wants a firm hand."* This is in the light of a previous occasion when his younger brother, Jack, was asked if he was a good boy to which

BELOW: *The 7th Duke and Duchess*

BOTTOM: *Winston's first letter to his mother, from Blenheim*

Soldiers and Flags and Castle they are so nice it was so kind you and dear ha I send you my love and a great many kisses Your loving Winston

My dear Mamma I hope you are quite well I thank you very very much for the beautiful presents those

4

RIGHT: *Winston aged seven*

he replied that he was but "*Winston is teaching me how to be naughty.*" Growing up with Blenheim as his backdrop inevitably created a self-assurance in the boy which marked the leader in later life.

Despite his privileged and confidence-building background Winston was not an academically promising child. In fact, his school reports were quite critical and showed him to be a mediocre student. Although he had ability he lacked the application and effort needed to flourish. However, he was always strong on history. We still have one of his Harrow exercise books where he writes at length his personal account of the Battle of Blenheim with his own carefully drawn maps. However, some general lessons had been learned and his last report from the headmaster at Harrow read, "*His work this term has been excellent. He understands now the need of taking trouble...*"

LEFT: *Letter to Mamma*

BELOW: *Map of the Battle of Blenheim drawn by Winston at Harrow*

"I am enjoying myself here very much it is so nice being in the country."

Military man

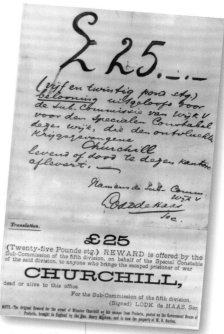

I N THE LIGHT of his high regard for the 1st Duke's military achievement, it is hardly surprising that Winston's ambition was the army and action. He entered Sandhurst in 1893 and wrote to his grandmother at Blenheim Palace: "*I have now been a full week at Sandhurst and like it very much indeed. There is a great deal of drill which is awfully fatiguing and I have a very uncomfortable room with two other boys but the work is very interesting – the food is good – and I have lots of my friends to associate with...*"

Churchill excelled at Sandhurst and was commissioned into the 4th Hussars in November 1895. He sought his mother's help through her society contacts to find attachment to units in more active service. He found action with the Spanish army in Cuba, with the Malakand Field Force on the north west frontier of India and, in the Sudan. Here, at Omdurman, with the 21st Lancers, he famously took part in the last regimental cavalry charge of the British army, narrowly escaping death himself although the trooper behind was killed.

"*For the first time that morning I experienced a sudden sensation of fear. I felt myself absolutely alone. I thought these riflemen would hit me and the rest devour me like wolves. What a fool I was to loiter like this in the midst of the enemy!*"

Like his great ancestor, John Churchill, 1st Duke of Marlborough, and perhaps following his example, Winston was a man of action, frequently risking himself in dangerous situations and, like the Duke, narrowly escaping death on more than one occasion. Destiny seemed to give him a charmed life.

When he left the army in 1899 he was assigned to cover the Boer War for the London *Morning Post*. Again he placed himself in danger in action with an armoured train and was promptly captured, only to escape with great daring – a reward of £25 was offered for his recapture. He found himself to be a celebrity on his return to England.

The energy and zest which characterised his conduct were noticed at this time at Blenheim where he was a frequent visitor. Writing later about those years, the American, Consuelo Vanderbilt, who had married Winston's cousin, 'Sunny', 9th Duke of Marlborough, described "*...a young red-headed boy a few years older than I. He struck me as ardent and vital and seemed to have every intention of getting the most out of life, whether in sport, in love, in adventure or in politics*". This was Winston.

ABOVE: *Winston and Consuelo, 9th Duchess*

LEFT: *Winston with his squadron in the Kitchen Court at Blenheim Palace*

The Member of Parliament for Oldham

In this temple Winston S. Churchill proposed to Clementine Hozier 11th August 1908

Love and marriage...

IN 1900 WINSTON was elected MP for Oldham, yet despite a busy political life, with characteristic energy he readily found time to produce his first major book, significantly Blenheim based, publishing *Lord Randolph Churchill*, an acclaimed biography of his father, in 1906.

In the book he brings out again his strong sense of the continuity of history he felt at Blenheim, his feeling there of a grand scheme of things. *"The antiquity of Woodstock"*, he wrote, *"is not measured by a thousand years and Blenheim is heir to all the memories of Woodstock."*

Churchill's personal circumstances were now about to change radically. *"At Blenheim"*, he wrote, *"I took two important decisions: to be born and to marry. I am happily content with the decisions I took on both occasions"*. In August 1908, Miss Clementine Hozier was invited as a guest to Blenheim because it was there, quite deliberately, that Churchill wished to propose to her. When he rose too late for their morning meeting, only the timely intervention of his cousin, the 9th Duke, who took Miss Hozier for a carriage ride, prevented this strong-minded woman from departing for London immediately. However, Winston eventually arrived in time to forestall this.

Their pleasant walk in the gardens was interrupted by rain and so they found shelter in the nearby Temple of Diana. Uncharacteristically, Churchill's confidence and loquacity deserted him. He seemed so unable to get to the point that Clementine, as she recorded later, decided that if an insect on the floor reached a nearby crack and he still had not proposed then she would leave him to it. However, the words were found, the answer was given and all was well.

LEFT: *Clementine Hozier at the time of her engagement*　　INSET: *Plaque in the Temple of Diana*

Touching memories remain of this start of a love match which was to end only with Churchill's death 57 years later.

Such was the intensity of feeling between them, that in the happiness of their engagement they could not resist sending each other a number of notes internally along the Blenheim corridors, notes now in retrospect quite charming. On headed Blenheim notepaper, their lines exist to this day. One of Clementine's is particularly charming. She writes "*Je t'aime passionnement. I feel less shy in French.*" This correspondence continues over several loving notes.

They were married a month later, on 12th September 1908.

There is a further moving record in the Palace Visitor's Book. The list of guests at the engagement house party includes the signatures of CLEMENTINE HOZIER and Winston Churchill. Their honeymoon began at Blenheim and the very next entry, in her own hand, reads, CLEMENTINE S. CHURCHILL. Clearly Clementine wished to proclaim her married state – and her husband.

"My most brilliant achievement was to persuade my wife to marry me."

ABOVE: *Note written immediately after the engagement*

RIGHT: *The Visitors' Book entries*

BACKGROUND: *The Temple of Diana*

The Four Churchills (left to right) Winston; Jack (Winston's brother); 9th Duke; Viscount Churchill

The Duke of Marlborough's Own

CHURCHILL'S military career did not end when he resigned his commission in 1899. His involvement in military life continued, now, not surprisingly, in connection with Blenheim. He joined the county territorial cavalry regiment, The Queen's Own Oxfordshire Hussars. Such was the strength of the Blenheim connection that the regiment was known locally as "The Duke of Marlborough's Own". Serving with Winston were Sunny, the 9th Duke, Winston's brother, Jack, and Viscount Churchill of Cornbury Park. Churchill himself commanded a squadron and even in his busy time as Home Secretary he was an active and efficient commanding officer. He maintained his connection with the regiment throughout his life. On Queen Mary's death in 1953 Churchill became Colonel in Chief of the Regiment, a position he held until his death and, at his request, a contingent formed part of his funeral parade.

The exciting and dramatic times were those spent in annual camp, often in Blenheim Park. In 1911 it produced this revealing event. He wrote to Clementine:

"6 June 1911 Blenheim.
My dearest,
We all marched past this morning — walk, trot and gallop. Jack and I took our squadrons at real pace and excited the spontaneous plaudits of the crowd... after the march past I made the general form the whole Brigade into Brigade Mass and galloped 1,200 strong the whole length of the park in one solid square of men and horses. It went awfully well. He was delighted".

This must have been the first time in the history of the British army that a major made a general do anything.

"Courage is the first of all human qualities because it generates all others."

Winston with his squadron at full gallop in Blenheim Park 1911

The Long Library

Maturing politician...

CHURCHILL'S early years in Government reveal a true social conscience characterised by much effective action to relieve deprivation. The all pervasiveness of Blenheim in Churchill's life is witnessed by a vivid and pointed Max Beerbohm cartoon, which hangs at Blenheim to this day, showing Churchill and his cousin, the 9th Duke. In 1910, rather against the interests of his own class, Churchill had been a staunch supporter of Lloyd George's 'People's Budget' which raised considerable new taxes, partly at the expense of the landed class, to finance large-scale social reform.

The cartoon shows a smiling Churchill speaking with teasing reassurance to his cousin, the Duke. *"Come, come, as I said in one of my speeches, there is nothing in the budget to make it harder for a poor, hard-working man to keep a small home in the country"*. Behind them in the cartoon stands Blenheim Palace.

As Churchill's status and confidence as a national figure developed through his thirties, the importance of Blenheim continued, sometimes in less than obvious ways. The oral record from an estate family highlights one part that Blenheim played.

A retired Blenheim staff member tells of his father stamping into their estate cottage some 80 years ago at 3 o'clock in the morning muttering darkly about Churchill's habitual late evenings. Churchill's delight after dinner was to gather guests around him in the Long Library, where he gleaned knowledge and experience from political, business and financial leaders and established his own influence. Night owl that he was, he was oblivious of the fact that for so long as he stayed there the Palace engineer had to remain on duty at the generator which at that time provided the lighting thus arriving home in the early hours not in the best of tempers, as his son indelibly remembered.

During the Great War, Churchill, as First Lord of the Admiralty, Lt. Col. in command of the Royal Scots Fusiliers in the trenches and Secretary of State for War, was of necessity detached from Blenheim – but not totally.

A revealing letter dated March 1918 has recently been discovered in the archives after lying undisturbed for many years. As Secretary of State for War, visiting the trenches on the Western Front, Churchill writes to his cousin, the 9th

ABOVE: *Winston the orator in full flow. Cartoon from Vanity Fair (1911)*

RIGHT: *The 9th Duke and Consuelo with their two sons. By John Singer Sargent (1905)*

BELOW: *Letter from Winston as Secretary of State for War to the 9th Duke on meeting his son in the trenches (1918)*

Duke, saying he had come across his son (later the 10th Duke) at the front with his men. In Churchillian prose he describes the scene: the mud, horses and tents, the artillery overhead, and adds that the young man is well and safe. Then, with typical humour states, *"He looked very well, and quite happy, and was I think agreeably surprised by the sudden advent of an avuncular relation"*.

This is not the Secretary of State for War writing to a Duke about a future Duke. Rather it is a letter to a father whose son is in danger in the trenches, assuring him of the young man's safety. The insight into Churchill's humanity, compassion and warmth is what is so revealing here.

Painting as a pastime

SHORTLY AFTER THE WAR, Churchill made one of his most radical personal decisions – in 1922 he bought Chartwell, where he would live for the next 43 years, until his death. At this house too, he revealed his devotion to Blenheim in several ways, none more telling than a detail in the decoration of his study. There, at the end of the room is the desk at which he worked and above which was hung a large painting of his inspiration through life, Blenheim Palace. This was the picture he looked at while working on his official papers as well as many of his major literary works including *The Second World War* and *A History of the English Speaking Peoples*. The Blenheim theme was also continued in his London house at 28 Hyde Park Gate, where, in the dining room this time, was hung a dramatic painting of the 1st Duke of Marlborough at the Battle of Blenheim.

Churchill himself did not take up painting until he was 41 and "*Blenheim provided an infinity of subjects*" (Lady Soames). He painted both Park and Palace although his preference seems to have been for the

"Painting is complete as a distraction. I know of nothing which, without exhausting the body, more entirely absorbs the mind..."

BELOW: *This dramatic painting of the Battle of Blenheim hung in Winston's dining room at Hyde Park Gate for the last 20 years of his life. By the Circle of Adam Frans van der Meulen (c. 1712)*

interior of this great house, perhaps because here he could best reflect the achievements of the 1st Duke which affected him so much.

Certainly two of his most notable paintings are of the interior and relate to the campaigns of the Duke. Churchill's luxuriant painting of the large Bouchain tapestry (the Duke's last and particularly dramatic action) was judged by the art critic, Thomas Bodkin, to be possibly Churchill's best interior.

In 1928 Winston was painting the Great Hall in the Palace which is dominated by the great arch symbolising the 1st Duke's victory at Blenheim. Mary, the 10th Duchess, passed and admired what he was doing. "*You like it, Mary,*" he said "*then you shall have it*" and have it she did. When it was completed he gave it to her and it hangs at Blenheim to this day. The impetuosity and generosity were typical of him.

The most important Blenheim-related event for Churchill in the inter war years followed his loss of office in 1929 when he began his Wilderness Years. He came to Blenheim where his cousin, the 9th Duke, provided accommodation and allowed him privileged access to the Blenheim archive, the vast store of historic documents from which he wrote *Marlborough His Life and Times*, a powerful and acclaimed biography of his great ancestor. In it he sums up the Duke's victory at the Battle of Blenheim memorably as having "*changed the political axis of the world*".

TOP LEFT:
*The Boathouse and Lake
at Blenheim*

TOP RIGHT:
*The Great Hall,
given by Churchill to Mary,
the 10th Duchess*

RIGHT:
The Bouchain Tapestry

BELOW LEFT:
Cannon Point

BELOW RIGHT:
*The West Front of
Blenheim Palace*

*"Blenheim is
immortal as
a battle...
because it
changed the
political axis of
the world.."*

Winston Churchill [signature]

ABOVE: *Winston outside Number 10*

Destiny realised...

ON 10TH MAY 1940 Churchill became Prime Minister and things looked bleak as Britain stood alone in Europe in the path of the Nazi menace. Yet now his sense of destiny, which Blenheim had done so much to nurture, reached its height.

"I was conscious of a profound sense of relief. At last I had the authority to give directions over the whole scene. I felt as if I were walking with destiny, and that all my past life had been but a preparation for this hour and for this trial."

His task was daunting as virtually the whole of Europe was to fall and setback followed setback throughout the world. Three of the strengths particularly of this multi-talented man emerged to meet the crisis. His personal courage founded a resistance in the face of these apparently insurmountable odds. His remarkable energy, especially in a man of 65, made his presence felt in every aspect of the allied effort (he travelled 150,000 international miles in the course of the war). Most importantly, his capacity to inspire bolstered the morale of the nation. Great lines from his speeches are now part of the nation's heritage:

"We shall fight them on the beaches...we shall never surrender."

"Blood, toil, tears and sweat."

"Never in the field of human conflict has so much been owed by so many to so few."

A statement in Latin on the roof of Blenheim Palace describes the 1st Duke as *Protector of the Freedom of Europe*. How amazingly apt a description is this also of his great descendant, Winston.

He had little time for Blenheim for the next five years but connections, however slight, remained. For example, when the premises of Malvern College were needed for government purposes he was instrumental in the relocation of several hundred schoolboys to Blenheim. On the occasions he stayed at Ditchley Park, he took the opportunity to motor across to Blenheim. On a cold November day in 1941 he gave a 15-year-old schoolboy a memorable experience when he took his godson, Sunny Marlborough, later the 11th Duke, to Liverpool where Churchill's presence gave a much deserved boost to the morale of the people of that badly bombed city.

Churchill's most powerful legacy is of having saved Europe from Nazi domination. This is a striking parallel

RIGHT: *John Churchill, the 1st Duke of Marlborough. By John Closterman*

"He mobilised the English language and sent it into battle to steady his fellow countrymen and hearten those Europeans upon whom the long dark night of tyranny had descended."
– Ed Murrow

LEFT: *Winston as wartime Prime Minister, visiting Liverpool with his godson (the present Duke) 1941*

with the 1st Duke who freed Europe from French control. It is perhaps the strongest of a range of parallels between the two men: there are numerous others. Both were brought from the political wilderness by a world conflict – John Churchill by the War of the Spanish Succession, Winston Churchill by World War II. Both were professional soldiers who had narrow escapes from death in action – John in Brabant in 1705 and again at Ramillies in 1706, Winston many times, famously at Omdurman. Both rose above the mere action of war into being effective statesmen, realising vital partnerships with their allies. Both achieved distinction late in life – John in his fifties and Winston aged 65. Both produced resounding victories but were then disregarded by their countrymen – John was impeached on trumped up charges of embezzlement of army funds and dismissed, Winston uncere- moniously lost the 1945 election and his premiership after the war. But, both also recovered from their setbacks – John was restored to all honours by King George I and Winston was returned to power in 1951.

Last resting place

IN HIS FIVE YEARS as Leader of the Opposition, Winston turned to Blenheim once again, in August 1947. Having received the Freedom of Woodstock in the morning, in the afternoon he spoke at the Conservative Party rally of 40,000 staged for him by the 10th Duchess on the South Lawn of the Palace.

The BBC World Service broadcast Winston's speech in which there were two themes: acknowledgement of a debt of gratitude to the United States for their help in the recent war and, unbelievably prophetically, a conviction that the means of preventing future European conflict was to break down national boundaries and create a more united Europe.

Eighteen years after this prophetic moment came the final contact with Blenheim. Sir Winston died on 24th January 1965. A few days later, on the 30th, he had the rare honour for a commoner of a state funeral.

"The nation had the lion's heart. I had the luck to give the roar."

RIGHT: *Extract from the 1947 speech at Blenheim*

BELOW: *The Freedom of Woodstock scroll signed by Mary, the 10th Duchess*

OPPOSITE: *The last resting place for Winston and Clementine in the churchyard at Bladon*

From Long Hanborough station, he was brought to the quiet country chuchyard at Bladon, to be buried among his family, less than a mile from the tomb and monument of his great hero and inspiration, John, 1st Duke of Marlborough – at Blenheim Palace.

The whole English-speaking world must move forward together in fraternal association along the lines of destiny.

This will be the gtst hope of peace among nations and, of the freedom and dignity of ordinary men and women over the largest portion of the globe.

The conception of United Europe joined together in amity and fact, though not perhaps at first in form,

in no way conflicts w the fraternal association of the English-speaking Commonwealths and States.

On the contrary, both these natural and vital affiliations are drawn together in their due subordination to the supreme U.N.O., and can only be contributory parts of the world system.